Love Will Find Your Home

Adam Starks, PhD

Illustrated by
Natasha Payne-Brunson

ISBN 979-8-218-41304-0 (paperback)
ISBN 979-8-218-41305-7 (digital)

Printed in the United States of America

*This book is dedicated to my brothers
Noah and Chris. We made it!
I also want to dedicate this book to my long-lost
brother, Moses. I hope to someday embrace you again.
Lastly, I'd like to dedicate this book to my brother
Matthew and any half-siblings of my unknown
father's side. I don't have to know you to love you.*

My mommy couldn't take care of me, and Daddy
left me. Love, can you find me a home?

Here is your home, little one, with a loving father
and mother who will always be here for you.

My daddy abused me, and I need to feel protected. Love, can you find me a home?

Here is your home, little one, with a loving
father and mother to protect you.

My mommy and daddy used drugs and didn't feed me. Love, can you find me a home?

Here is your home, little one, where the food
is plentiful, and our hearts are pure.

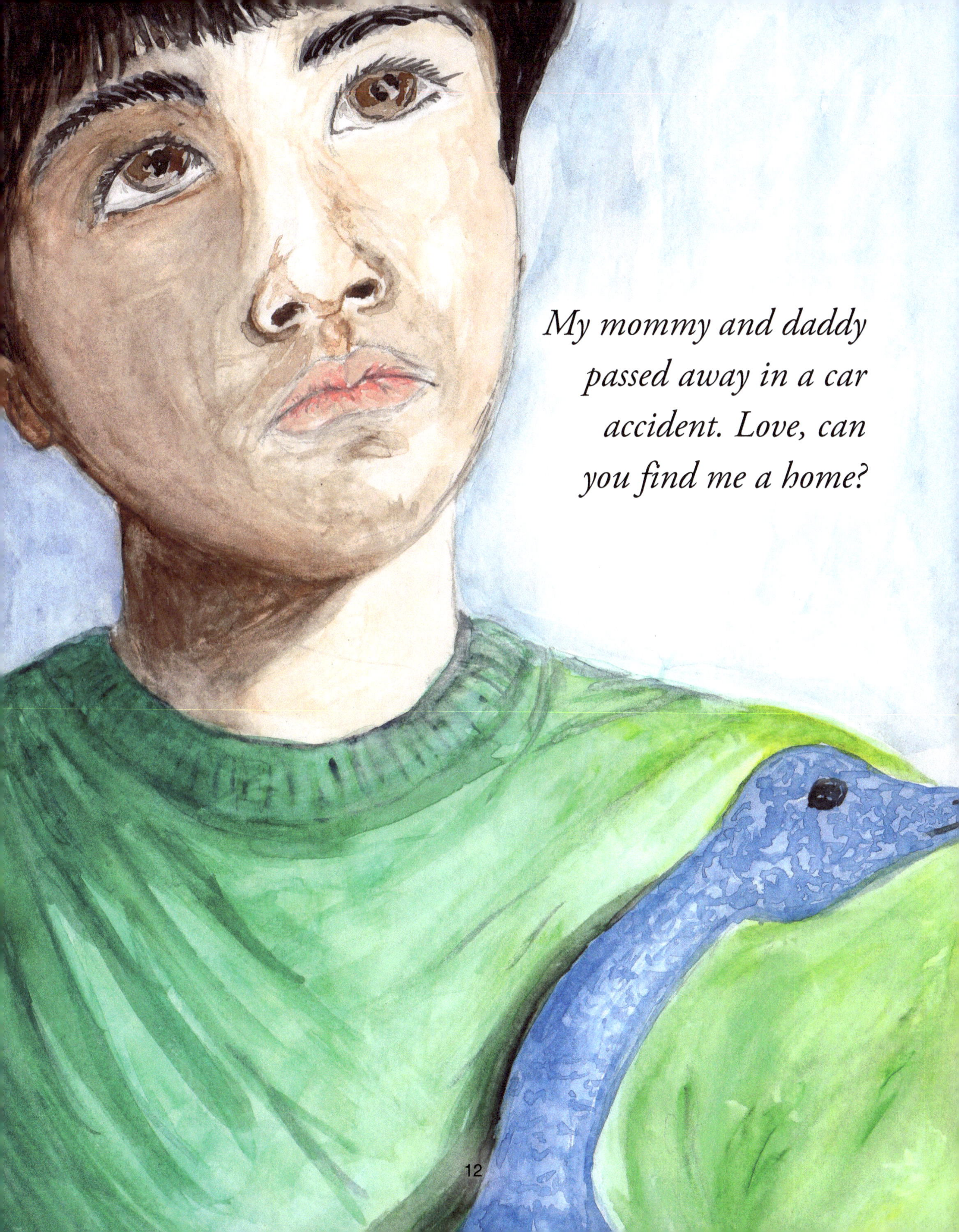

My mommy and daddy
passed away in a car
accident. Love, can
you find me a home?

Here is your new home, little one, where
we will always honor your parents by
loving you as much as they did.

My mommy and daddy tried to sell me to a stranger. Love, can you find me a home?

Here's your new home, little one. Your
innocence will always be safe here.

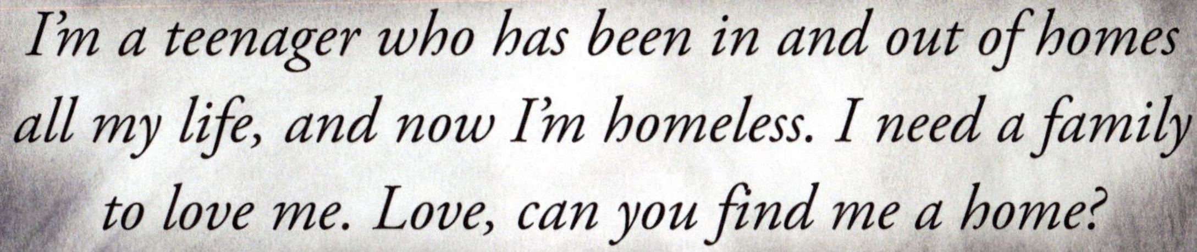

I'm a teenager who has been in and out of homes all my life, and now I'm homeless. I need a family to love me. Love, can you find me a home?

Here is your forever home, young man, where we'll provide the loving guidance you need to spread your wings in this uncertain world.

I can't talk yet, but I was abandoned and found in a trash dumpster behind the school. Love, can you find me a home?

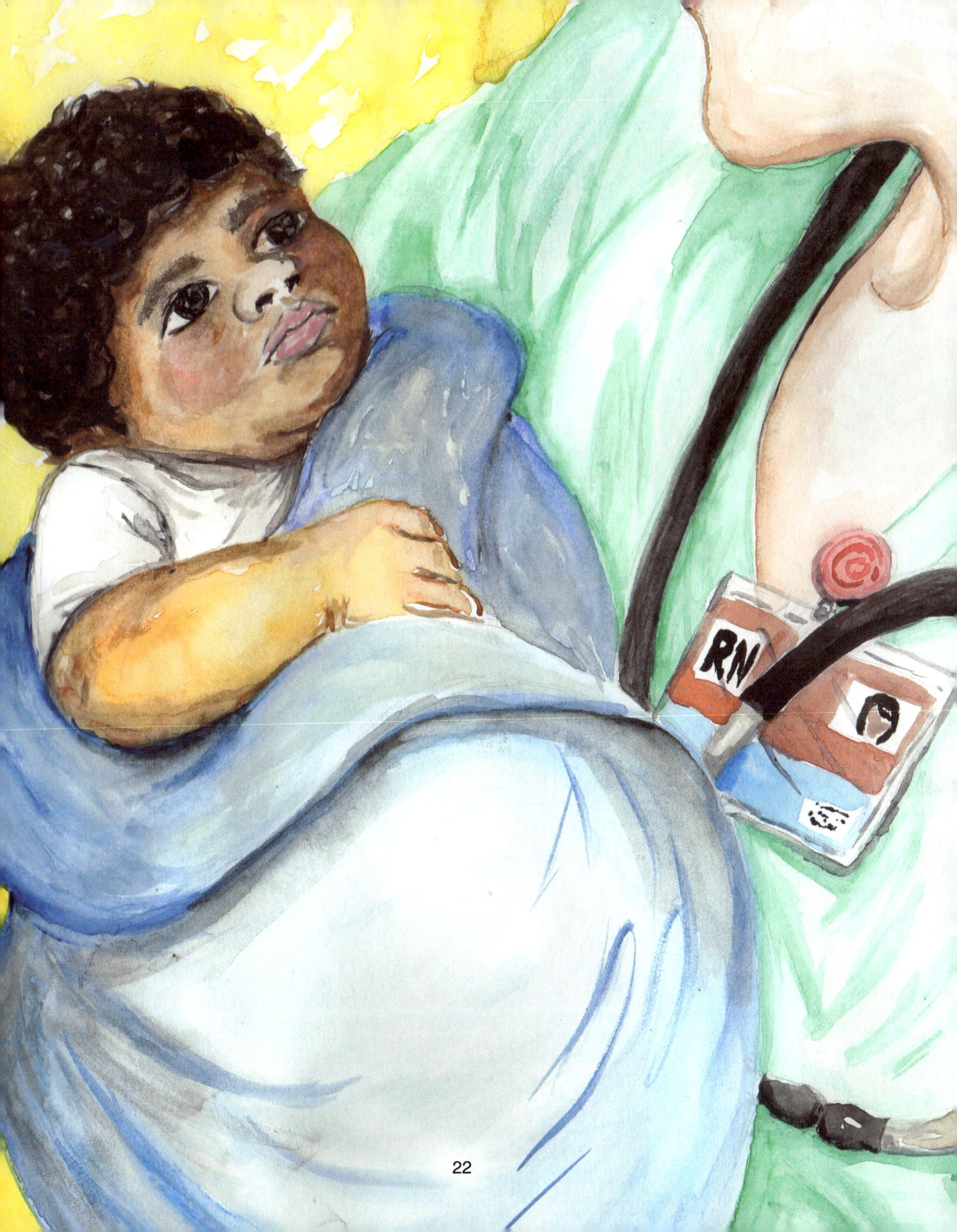

22

Welcome to your new home, little one.
We will never, ever abandon you.

This is our home.
I promise you the safety and security
that comes with being loved.

25

You will never be neglected physically, mentally, or any other way. No matter what happens, we will always cherish you.

Rest easy. Dream brightly. You are loved.

About the Author

Dr. Adam Starks is a former foster child and author of *Broken Child Mended Man: An Autobiography*. Dr. Starks and his siblings grew up in abject poverty in rural Virginia. However, Adam's story is not your typical account of a foster child who went on to beat the odds. Dr. Starks went on to study Business Administration at Eastern Mennonite University, earn an MBA at Strayer University, and a PhD in Organizational Leadership from Capella University.

Dr. Starks has an important message to share with foster parents, foster care professionals, and educators: "Don't ever give up on us!" Dr. Starks believes his positive foster care experience and the adult outcome can be replicated when foster parents, social workers, and educators understand the intricacies and importance of their roles raising healthy foster youth and preparing them for adulthood. He also delivers a powerful personal message to current foster youth preparing for emancipation by instilling a message of embracing community and self-discovery. To request keynote speaking engagements or for more info, please visit adamstarks.com.

About the Illustrator

Natasha Payne-Brunson is a librarian by trade, and she enjoys spending her spare time working on illustrations and graphic designs. She holds a Bachelor of Fine Arts degree in painting and printmaking from Virginia Commonwealth University and a Master of Science in Library Science from Clarion University. She is known as the "artsy librarian" and resides with her husband and two boys in Richmond, Virginia. Natasha can be contacted at npbrunsondesigns@gmail.com.